D1549812

What the Papers
Didn't Say

and Other Broadcast Talks

Colin Morris

COLIN MORRIS

What the Papers Didn't Say

and other Broadcast Talks

London EPWORTH PRESS

Printed and bound in
Great Britain by
C. Nicholls & Company Ltd
SBN 7162 0193 3

This book is for
ROY TREVIVIAN
who taught me
the game

Contents

Introduction

THE SPOKEN word when served up in print can be as unappetising as cold potatoes. It not only lacks urgency but also that peculiar flavour which any speaker conveys to his hearers not so much by what he says as by what he is. There is also a transient topicality about broadcasting which rarely survives the cold light of tomorrow's dawn. There is nothing quite so dead as yesterday's crisis. So I have chosen only those talks which, though geared to events of a given moment, deal, in my view, with perennial aspects of the human situation.

Two of the talks contained in this volume 'Do It Now!' and 'The Yes Beyond Yes and No' I later expanded into sermons which are printed in *Mankind Is My Church*, published by Hodder and Stoughton. And 'What's In a Word?' is owed to a theme by the late Dr F. W. Boreham in a volume of addresses which got lost somewhere in my move from Africa to London.

What I owe to the Religious Broadcasting Department of the BBC and in particular to the Producer of 'Thought for the Day' is acknowledged in the dedication of this book. But I would like to put on record my gratitude to Albert Jakeway, General Manager of the Methodist Book Room for much kindness, shrewd judgement and the gift of true friendship. Never was so skilled a publisher afflicted with so wayward an author – and survived!

COLIN M. MORRIS
Wesley's Chapel
London

Bias Be Blowed!

MY CRITICS were quite right. I *am* biased. In fact, I'm a seething mass of full-blooded prejudices. So are most of us. Show me somebody who is devoid of any form of bias and whose every response is measured, precise and balanced, and I'll show somebody who is a juiceless, colourless nonentity.

One way of summing up a personality is to analyse his biases – those instinctive judgements he makes about people or things in the heat of the moment, or the opinions which linger on in the deep recesses of his mind in the face of a mountain of facts to the contrary.

For example, I'm biased against television interviewers who invite people to their programmes in order to give them the third degree and then chop them off in mid-sentence and rush with indecent haste to the next item, presumably on the grounds that the poor, stupid viewers cannot be expected to concentrate on any subject for more than three and a half minutes. This seems to me to betray the ultimate contempt for the public intelligence.

I'm also biased against the great army of nosey parkers who reserve the right to stop us in the street, invade our homes, check our credit rating

11

and generally strip us naked in order to feed the maw of those data-banks which will form the pantheon of gods in the goldfish-bowl world of the future. There are those dolly birds who simper up to one in airports and ask all kinds of impertinent questions claiming that it will enable some airline to provide a more efficient service, by which I presume they mean maximise its profits at the expense of my right to keep to myself the reason for my journey, the size of my salary and the number of grandchildren I have. If I've got to choose, give me privacy over efficiency any day.

And I must confess to being psychotically biased against all forms of hunting, particularly when the devotees of the sport compound a felony of matching themselves in truly heroic odds – fifty dogs and twenty-five riders against a single fox – by assuring me what splendid fun the fox is having. Possibly some of them ought to volunteer to spend an afternoon on foot amongst the lions at Longleat so that they can tell us at first hand what fun it is to be hunted by real experts.

Some newspapers bring out all my insipient biases, especially Sunday newspapers which pay exhorbitant sums for the exclusive memoirs of some poor mutt whose only claim to immortality is that he or she has committed some grotesque and monumental folly. That's bad enough, but the clincher is that invariable statement as an introduction to the first article which tells me that I am being treated to an expensive journey through the sewers of society not to feed my appetite for pornography but as a public service and a salutory exercise in morality by courtesy of the newspaper proprietor.

I also have my biases in favour of things. I'm biased in favour of all characters – those eccentrics who defy the grey-flannel suited anonymity of modern society by wearing gorgeous plumage or living in barrels or selling germ-free air. I wouldn't have the courage to do likewise but I envy those who have. And I also have a sneaking regard for those who give their lives and money to utterly hopeless causes, like the gent who is devoting all his wealth to founding a society for the abolition of the motor car or the pacifist group who want to bring the rebel regime in Rhodesia toppling by sending out squadrons of bombers to drop loads of daffodils over Salisbury.

Of course I'm biased. But I would claim to believe in a biased God. According to the Bible, God has a built-in bias in favour of those whom society regards as being of little account – the poor, the outcast, the prostitute. They go into the Kingdom first; the well-heeled, comfortable and conformist find the turnstiles loaded against them. It's hard, but there it is. What does the Magnificat say? 'The arrogant of heart and mind he has put to rout; he has brought monarchs down from their thrones, but the humble have been lifted high. The hungry he has satisfied with good things, the rich empty away.' If that isn't thundering bias, I don't know what is. The injured sparrow that falls to the ground, says Jesus, is not merely entitled to equal treatment with the flock of healthy ones winging through the upper air; it is shamelessly favoured. His kingdom is for the desperate, not the comfortable, and the army which marches behind him is largely composed of the barefooted legions of the poor and dispossessed.

So if I want to follow too, how can I help being biased?

What the Papers Didn't Say

To FOLLOW that popular feature of the *Today* programme 'What the Papers say', here is a companion piece on what the papers *didn't* say.

The mass circulation *Sun* this morning did not contain a full-page photo-feature on the vast majority of British ladies who prefer to keep their clothes *on* in public. Also missing was the sensational news that despite strains and stresses happy family life survives; that most teen-agers wouldn't know the difference between cannabis and caviar if their lives depended on it, and although their hair may be a little long for some headmasters' taste, they are in grave danger of growing up to be responsible citizens.

A long leader in the *Daily Express* did not say (and I quote) 'The public have been greatly inconvenienced by recent strikes. But don't let our annoyance blind us to the fact that for every trade unionist who hits the headlines as organiser of a strike, hundreds more spend hours of their own time, at their own expense, trying to prevent strikes. Thousands of industrial disputes are settled amicably each week around a table by these valuable public servants who fight for a fair deal for their members but also have a sense of responsibility to industry as a whole. Three cheers for these trouble-shooters of industry, who, together with dedicated managements, help to keep the wheels turning. Let's stop knocking them and support them in a tough job.'

The Communist *Morning Star* did not have as its main lead a protest about the dangers of too much freedom of expression in bourgeois Britain, and its Profile of the Week did not feature the capitalist who pays his workers a just wage, charges a reasonable price for his goods and when costs increase bears them out of his profit margins. The serialisation of the memoirs of Stalin has also been held over until someone in the Kremlin decides whether he is in or out.

Today's *Horse and Hound* has no article on 'The Joys of Hunting' No.1. – the Fox's Point of View. Badgers and baby seals are not expected to contribute future articles in the series.

There was no leader in this morning's *Financial Times* headed 'Money isn't everything' and pointing out that the quality of life in Britain is not finally dependent upon the index of share prices. Commenting on a report that a Kenyan football team had employed a witch-doctor to cancel the spells cast by a rival club, the writer did not go on 'Bearing in mind that share prices often fluctuate as a result of baseless rumour and speculation rather than hard fact, the Stock Exchange could do with the old Gospel power of exorcism to cast the demons out of our fiscal system and bring the power of money back under rational control.'

Private Eye this week had no exposé of the

business tycoon whose public and private lives are both beyond reproach, and the *Astrologer's Weekly* omitted to mention the case of the Capricornian for whom it predicted last week a full, long and satisfying life whose encounter with a steam roller yesterday somewhat depressed his prospects.

The *Daily Telegraph* this morning lacked a centre page spread devoted to a special article on the value of the Commonwealth and detailing the successes of newly independent African States in the fight, against great odds, to beat the old enemies of poverty, disease and ignorance. As the article does not conclude 'Let no-one sell the Commonwealth short. For all its failings, it is the fragile beginnings of a truly international community which transcends racial, cultural and religious barriers.' Also unreported was the story of the gang of immigrant youths who were not roaming the streets of Islington last night because they were busy painting out the house of a white old-age pensioner.

And none of the papers mentioned the fact that Jesus is alive and well and to be found wherever people are in need of forgiveness, healing and comfort.

The Sales Talk of a Bald-Headed Man

I HAVE a friend who periodically suffers from mother-in-law trouble, and when things reach the giddy limit, he gives vent to the anguished cry, 'I *like* the human race; all my family belong to it, and some of my wife's family belong to it as well!' Fair comment, I suppose, as a good natured jibe at one's mother-in-law, but in a more serious idiom it expresses an attitude which is at the root of many of Mankind's problems – 'All Whites belong to the Chosen Race, and a few Blacks do as well!', or 'All Protestants will be saved, and a few Catholics might slip through as well!' It's a form of tunnel vision – our inability to see anybody but our own kind. We even think, God help us, that it's one of our own kind who presides in Heaven. An African colleague once said to me, half jokingly, 'The trouble with you missionaries is that you think God is a white, English-speaking Methodist, when everyone knows he's a black, Swahili-speaking Anglican!'

All of which leads me to voice my anxiety for and sense of dedication to the Commonwealth, whose leaders are now engaged in a crucial meeting in Singapore. Because we suffer from tunnel vision where our fellow-men are concerned, we *need* some symbol of human togetherness which overarches our narrow nationalisms, racial arrogances and religious bigotries. Possibly it seems that what the Commonwealth stands for is too idealistic ever to be earthed in the real world; maybe we doubt that it is possible to harness together the strong and the weak, the rich and the poor for very long before the pride of the one and the resentment of the other tear them apart. Nevertheless, the Commonwealth is a working model of the brotherhood of Man. It has succeeded in throwing fragile bridges across the gulfs which divide men by race and religion and language. It is an honorable attempt to move beyond pious intentions towards the institutionalising of our hopes. Hence, it is not merely a symbol of some of Mankind's ultimate goals, but also a staging post on the road to their realisation.

As a Christian I believe that the essential unity of Mankind must sooner or later find political expression, not simply because it is clear that in the nuclear age the whole world is the smallest unit of survival. There is also the conviction that problems which have reached global proportions will only yield before a truly international will to solve them. And most important, only a truly united mankind can contain the majestic dimensions of God's love. Only the rich and varied gifts of *all* men can portray the true glory of Man. Of course I can love God in my own Church – but only a bit of him. Of course I can love my neighbours in my own land – but only an unrepresentative cross-section of them.

19

It makes hard sense for nations with a common history, however sordid some of that history might be, to seek a common destiny, but not on the basic of vapid sentimentality or a facile all-pals-together philosophy. There are tough issues of justice and human rights to be squarely faced and honestly harmonised. So the reality is likely to be much more modest than the vision of world brotherhood. Yet even in the political realm men cannot live without visions, and that represented by the Commonwealth is a vision worth cherishing.

Today also happens to be the first day of the Week of Prayer for Christian Unity, when all Christians are reminded that we have added the scandal of ecclesiatical tribalism to all the other barriers which divide men. It is absurd to suggest that the re-union of the Churches would, of itself, have more than a marginal effect upon a grievously splintered world. But it is surely a matter of elementary integrity that the *condition* of those who offer to men a Gospel of Reconciliation should match their *claims*.

After all, would *you* believe the sales talk of a bald-headed man selling hair restorer?

All Gas and Gaiters?

I SEE that the popular Television series 'All Gas and Gaiters' has moved to Radio Four this week. I must say I'm very partial to the pleasantly nutty goings-on in the Cathedral Close, featuring that nit Noot, his bumbling Bishop, the detestable Dean and the very arch Archdeacon. I don't believe for a second that it gets within miles of the truth about the pressures of life in the average Cathedral – at least none that I've ever witnessed – but it's good clean fun. Yet I suspect that some Christians will not be amused by such ecclesiastical comedies. They are so jealous for the Church's honour and dignity that they believe even good natured fun-poking at the sacred institution is in bad taste.

'Let's not take the mickey out of the Church!' they cry. I can't honestly say it's an argument that impresses me very much. Is it not a little sad that the descendants of those who faced hungry lions and flaming arrows with equanimity should wither before a gust of gently mocking satire? Or is the real cause for offence the fact that many satires on the Church, far from being pure fantasy, get uncomfortably close to the truth about the inanities of too much of our life?

Take, for instance, that satirical and some would say 'sick' comedian, the late Lenny Bruce. Commenting on a protest by American churchmen about the proliferation of pornographic films, he said he agreed with their protest so wholeheartedly that he had decided not to let his children see the latest of many Hollywood spectaculars on the life of Christ because he did not want them to grow up to be Jew-killers. And he added pointedly that he had never seen a so-called 'blue' film in which anyone got beaten to a pulp or roasted alive with napalm. A powerful plea, was it not, that possibly the Church is prone to get worked up about the wrong obscenities?

Clever satire is certainly a welcome change from the level of fun-poking which was once regarded as the only legitimate laugh you were allowed at the Church's expense – red-nosed music hall comedians in clerical garb intoning mock sermons beginning 'My dear Flock, whom I have so often fleeced!' and bad jokes about the Church Commissioners' slum properties and missionaries in cooking pots.

What in fact is happening is that the roseate hue of false sanctity which for too long enveloped the Church and obscured true judgement of its performance has blown away. Gone for ever is that world of private privilege where ladies got out their best china and warned Grandpa not to use any four letter words because the vicar was coming to tea. Society no longer allows the Church exemption from cold, hard scrutiny on account of its past glories.

It is now being judged, like any other institution, in terms solely of its effectiveness and usefulness. And I believe that even by the most rigorous or even cynical appraisal of its performance, the Church is not all gas and gaiters. She contributes compassion and service and hard thinking to the life of our time. Not that we have any right to expect thanks or praise. It is a very human pride which makes Christians long for popular esteem. Jesus promised only scorn and rejection and Paul advised his followers to become fools for Christ's sake. And if a fool doesn't expect to get laughed at, who does?

So by all means let T.V. or any other of the media take the mickey out of the Church and let Christians laugh, if a little ruefully, along with the rest. Nor ought we to get too steamed up if parody occasionally shades into blasphemy, for anyone who reads the Bible knows that there is a kind of back-handed acknowledgement of God in the most dreadful blasphemy that is not to be found in formal but empty respect.

After all, if what the Church believes is true, satire and laughter cannot do any harm. If it isn't true, then the Church may as well give men cause for laughter if she can offer them nothing more fundamental.

Ironmongery in Space,
Poverty on Earth

PREPARATIONS for another U.S. Moon shot are now nearing their climax. And however the epic journey goes, there can be no doubt that it will prove to be a miracle of technological skill and a saga of human courage and endurance. Far be it from me to sound a discordant note, but I wonder whether we Earthmen, however technically competent we are, have the moral right to venture out in conquest of the Universe when so much of our own planet remains untamed.

Whenever I see pictures of those gigantic rockets lifting ponderously yet majestically off their launching pads and shooting upwards and outwards into the bright, blue yonder, I can't help thinking of the trillions of dollars and roubles burning away whilst vast tracts of the Earth remain sunk in primitive squalor and two thirds of it population remain underfed.

What makes the whole thing even more morally dubious is that the astronomic cost of the Moon shots is duplicated because national pride demands that the Stars and Stripes must fly over more extra-terrestrial territory, and vice versa.

We haven't yet made a really serious attempt to mobilise technology to conquer the Earth. In the realm of medicine, universities and research foundations are starved of funds to seek out the causes of cancer and coronary thrombosis. We know precious little about mental disease and the problems of old age. World health bodies, on inadequate budgets, struggle on, trying to wipe out bilharzia and malaria, and we've not yet faced up to the challenge of finding new sources of food to sustain an exploding population.

Granted, some of our problems do not lie in the realm of the scientifically insoluble but are perpetuated by selfishness and considerations of economic advantage. But many others lurk in those dark areas of human ignorance which only costly research can illuminate.

So when we set foot on other planets, we shall not only be taking with us our technological know-how and national flags but also a whole spectrum of physical and social diseases ranging from the common cold to racial discrimination – scourges to which we proud Lords of the Universe are still subject in our own backyards.

Certainly, it can be retorted that the urge to venture into and conquer the unknown is one of the glories of Man and has created much of what we call progress. This I gladly acknowledge. But when a significant proportion of the world's wealth is dedicated to filling outer space with scrap iron, maybe it's time we reassessed our priorities.

Has a bitterly divided world the moral right to export its dissensions to another planet? Must we look forward to the Moon's Sea of Tranquillity being divided by barbed wire as U.S. and Russian

25

zones are set up? God help any poor Moonlings there may be! Before they know it, they will have U.S. Marines landing on their shores to contain the spread of lunar communism, and those antennae of theirs, which science fiction writers assure us stick out of their square heads instead of ears will be buzzing with Soviet 'capitalist-imperialist-aggression' propaganda.

Until we develop the maturity to live in understanding and amity on Earth, we shall only be raising on another planet a second Tower of Babel and sowing the seeds for a repetition of our own bloody history.

I'm well aware that to take this line is to open oneself to the charge of having a Luddite mentality like those fellow north countrymen of mine who, during the Industrial Revolution, greeted the advent of the machine with orgies of destruction. So be it. I'm unrepentant. For me, the conquest of *inner* space comes first. Let's raise the flag of humanity over those vast areas of the Earth where men still live in slavery to the perennial enemies of poverty, disease and ignorance. Then we can start throwing our weight around the universe.

But until that time – even though it's a minority view – I don't think the entire space programme is worth the life of a single hungry child.

The Champion Who Came Second

UNTIL a few months ago, the average man, only mildly interested in sport probably knew the name of Lillian Board, who died this week of cancer, as the girl who came second in the most important race of her life – the 1968 Olympics. And if God has blessed us with any sensitivity at all, we must recognize what a peculiar martyrdom it is for a great athlete to finish second in any great sporting event. To win is to vindicate promise, to set the seal on fame and immortality. There's even a perverse sort of satisfaction for some people in spectacular failure – no one would ever be quite sure whether they were mere also-rans outclassed or world-beaters slightly off-form. But to run second – to give everything you've got, and for it to be not quite enough on the day; to know that you could have won, and didn't – that's a hard truth with which to live.

You find silver medallists in every walk of life – politicians who make the Cabinet but miss 10 Downing Street by a hair's breadth; actors playing supporting roles who might have been stars; people who, but for the quirks of fate, might have written a glowing page in the history books. To live with promise unfulfilled is to know the bitter frustration of a Captain Scott who battled across Antarctica against unbelievable odds and finally forfeited his life knowing he was the *second* man to reach the South Pole.

That silver medal is the most poignant of all awards. It usually identifies those who are undeniably great but miss being the greatest by an inch or a foot or a fraction of a second. I suppose it's not too hard to bear when you know all along that second place is the best you could justly hope for – one can show a certain equanimity then – but to be worthy of a 'gold' as Lillian Board was – and only to get a 'silver', that is to plumb the depths of despair.

Some might have remembered Lillian only as the girl who came second had it not been that out of due time she found herself in a grimmer contest, against terrifying odds; a struggle she could only win by refusing to break; by confronting the sordid and horrible with dignity and cheerfulness. To keep on fighting, not to some arbitrary finishing tape but to the bitter end – *usque ad mortem* – right up to death – that is a contest of a different order. Who now remembers the silver medal? In the supreme test she gained a triumphant First.

It would be fitting if at her Memorial Service they were to read that passage in St John's Gospel about the discovery of the empty tomb on Easter morning. It contains this little detail – 'So Peter and the other disciples set out for the tomb; they ran side by side, but the second disciple outran Peter and reached the tomb first.' Peter beaten into second place in what he must have thought was the most important race of his life! But it wasn't. The day came when Peter was called upon to share his Master's fate, which he did with shining faith. Peter the disciple who came second transformed a silver medal into a golden crown by enduring to the end – *usque ad mortem* – right up to death.

In a time plagued by prognostications of doom and crisis, when things seem to be in the saddle and ride men, we badly need the resplendent example that Lillian Board has left us. Possibly we've been so busy bewailing our miserable lot that we had almost forgotten that being human in the last resort is about courage and dignity and hope in the face of impossible odds; its about enduring triumphantly in circumstances where you cannot win.

Lillian Board will rest in the peace reserved for those whose spirits have been tempered in the flame of adversity; who fought on *usque ad mortem* and so enriched all humanity.

What better way could there be for a champion to set the record straight, once and for all?

The Brick With Your Name On It

I WAS a great admirer of Bertrand Russell. One of my cherished possessions is a newspaper cutting of a photograph of Bertrand Russell at an advanced age being marched off to prison for his part in a demonstration against nuclear weapons. Whether he was right or wrong about the issue is beside the point. The intriguing question is: why did he bother? Why was he prepared to suffer for something which could not possibly affect him personally? He must have known that the chances were that he would not still be alive on that terrible day when someone might press the red button which could take the world off its hinges.

Russell himself gave the answer when he wrote somewhere 'It is necessary to care deeply about things which will not come to pass until long after we are gone'. He made no claim to be a Christian but it would be difficult to find a more eloquent illustration of what Paul in his Letter to Timothy calls 'laying a good foundation for the future'.

Man is neither a superior species of vegetable nor a walking stomach. He can live on beyond his biological dissolution in a number of ways, one of which is the quality of the causes for which he stands. His unique dignity encompasses not only a debt to the past but also a responsibility for the future. He is able so to live in the present that when the final structure of things stands revealed long after he is gone, there is one brick with his name on it, just as the foundations of a world freed from the threat of nuclear extinction will include a corner-stone with Bertrand Russell's name graven across it.

In classical theology, pride is man's besetting sin. I suspect that cruelty rather than pride is the besetting sin of the modern world. But not far behind slinks another sin – the sin of triviality. Never in the history of the world has such a wealth of technical resource and human ingenuity been dedicated to such paltry, trivial purposes. A strong sense of responsibility for the future has given place to the vague hope that things will hold together for our life-time and possibly that of our children. Beyond that, let the chips fall where they may!

Yet had it not been for men and women prepared to lay a good foundation for the future by caring deeply for things which could not possibly come to pass until long after they were gone, we should still be living in caves, at the mercy of the elements, our minds darkened by fear and superstition.

To be truly human is to stand for causes which will not exhaust themselves before we exhaust ourselves. None are so pathetic as those who have outlived the causes to which they have given their lives. Eaten away by nostalgia, they linger on, like the rusting equipment of some long-abandoned

31

experiment. The cause has got to be bigger than the man. What is the point of creating man capable of dreams if he has nothing to dream about: if his reach does not exceed his grasp?

All right, so I am not going to see the great scourges of mankind – poverty, discrimination, injustice, war – irradicated in my life-time or even in the lifetime of my chldren and my children's children. But I'm not going to lie down and bemoan the futility and wickedness of life. I can take one tiny step, strike one feeble blow, lay one small brick on behalf of the future.

So God's kingdom tarries and things seem to drag on in the same old way. Men and nations resist God's grace and history seems to be as opaque to meaning as ever. But there is one bit of creation I have the power to change, to transform into the stuff of the future. Or at least, *I* can't transform it, but I can, by acknowledging God's rule over my life, become an outpost of the new society – tomorrow's world.

To lay a good foundation for the future is to stand for causes which are unlikely to achieve fulfilment until long after we are gone. It is no trivial immortality to be able to claim that we stood for the Kingdom in the day of small things. We did the truth, lived by love, refused to give up hope and so created the raw material of a good future. That is how the most ordinary life can achieve significance, and the bonus is the assurance that in the final edifice of things – that new heaven and new earth – there will be one small brick with your name upon it.

Who Dun It?—And How?

I'M A FAILED writer of detective stories. I've never quite got the hang of the art. Either I start writing from the beginning and by the time I reach the final chapter I've collected a couple of characters on the way I just can't account for, or else I try writing backwards from the unmasking of the villain to the committing of the crime and find that although my solution is plausible the crime is quite impossible. It just couldn't have been done that way. Or worse, the villain was in Edinburgh when the victim met his grisly end in Birmingham.

A friend of mine in the publishing world told me how it should be done. He claims that in every good detective story there is one chapter fairly near the end where the character of the villain undergoes a subtle transformation. He says or does something which reveals that he isn't what he seems to be. He is exposed as the sort of person who could have committed the crime. Then having nailed down the villain's character, the author writes backwards from that chapter to the crime and forwards to its solution.

Well, I've never tried it, but I do find that explanation useful when I attempt to puzzle out the account in Genesis of the creation of the world. There were, after all, no eye-witnesses of this event, so how did those old Hebrews who wrote Genesis know how it was done? If we assume that they were responsible men who did not indulge in flights of poetic fancy for its own sake, there can only be one explanation.

Like the detective story writer, they took as their starting point not a series of events but a character. They concentrated upon the Creator of whom they had some first-hand knowledge rather than upon the Creation of which they had none. They must have asked themselves: how would the God we know *now* have acted *then*?

Once they'd got the character of the Creator clear in their minds from personal experience, they then wrote backwards to the Creation, confident that God's nature had remained consistent throughout recorded time.

So the Creation story is not an exercise in pseudo-science. It tells us less about how things were at the very beginning than about what God meant to the writers in their own time. And if the Creation story speaks of order, trust and love being at the heart of things, it is because the men who wrote that account had found God in their own experience utterly trustworthy, consistent and loving.

But there's one odd detail in this Genesis creation story. It is the only one known to me where it is claimed that God created the world *out of nothing*. In the creation myths of other religions, there is always an original substance out of which God fashioned the world – fire or water or whatever. It's worth asking why the Hebrews made this affirmation.

The answer, I suppose, is that every artist is limited by the nature of the material with which he must work. A great sculptor or painter can do amazing things with stone or paint. But he cannot do *anything* he chooses with them. Beyond a certain point the material the artist uses becomes resistant to his will. This is equally true of the words which the writer or speaker uses. To a certain point he can express his thoughts with precision, but beyond that point he finds words and syntax and grammar putting limits upon what he wants to say. Didn't Shakespeare write over a hundred sonnets on the meaning of love, and no doubt even at the very end he must have felt that he hadn't quite succeeded.

On the other hand, if God created the world out of nothing, this must mean that there was no original material to set limits upon what he could do. There was nothing to resist his will or restrict his artistic imagination. And this is no rarefied truth. It means that the world must be basically exactly how God intended it to be – a good world, and if you retort, as you are entitled to, that it's become pretty misshapen by evil, then this evil must be seen as an alien interloper which had no part in the original scheme of things. Nor can it in the last resort frustrate God's plans.

And what about Man? He, too, is part of this Creation which God made out of nothing. So he must be basically good and capable of infinite possibilities. But there is an important condition which he must meet before he can truly take his place as the crown of creation. The God who created the world out of nothing can't do much with us unless we too become nothing – humble, teachable and open to God's will. As Jesus said, it is the poor in spirit, those without false illusions of independence, of overweaning pride; those, in fact, who are nothing, and know it, to whom the Kingdom belongs.

Homo Telegensis

I'VE BEEN reading this week-end about an American sociologist who claims that if an invader from another planet wanted to find out how Earthman ticks, the best thing he could do would be to study television commercials. These, he suggests, are the modern equivalent of those cave drawings from which we have learned so much about our own ancestors.

So I dutifully watched my television set to see how Earthman, let's call him Joe Bloggs (no reference intended, needless to say, to anyone, living or dead, by that name) would appear to a visitor from Mars. The mind boggles!

Joe Bloggs has a wife and two kids, one of whom must be illiterate because he spends his time going around reciting corny poetry in praise of Keen's beans when he should be at school. They also have a big dog who leaves dirty paw marks on the kitchen floor and turns up his nose at any dog food which isn't fortified by at least 27 different vitamins like Tinnomeat. They live in a house which the bank manager they keep in a cupboard talked them into buying, surrounded by a high fence to hold off the hordes of soap powder representatives who descend to finger the family wash whilst husband is at work.

The house is always in a bit of a mess because when Mrs Bloggs isn't luxuriating in a bath imagining she's Olive Oyle or another of the nine out of ten film stars who use Lick soap, she's taking advantage of the milkman this Christmas. Poor fool! She doesn't realise that he's only there for the beer. In fact, Mrs Bloggs isn't very bright. Although her husband recognizes the shape of a good Scotch, she can't tell the difference between butter and margarine. Mind you, Bloggs wouldn't have been stuck with the dowdy creature in the first place if he'd started using Hari Kari aftershave lotion sooner. He'd have been fighting off that glamorous brunette who's so much stronger than he is because she starts her day with a big, fortifying Beetwix breakfast.

Britain's greatest problems are dandruff and a thirst that bites.

All her neighbours hate Mrs Bloggs because her washing is so much whiter than theirs, and she's clean round the bend thanks to Marpic. Her cooking, though, leaves much to be desired. She's so busy looking up in the dictionary words like hexachlorzene, diadin and other mystery ingredients of her toothpaste that she's reduced to opening a tin of steaming Lorco soup when guests arrive for dinner – which isn't often because they generally leave her house clutching their stomachs and are only saved from a fatal attack of peritonitis by a sparkling glass of fizzy Emus.

The Bloggs children are frightful little know-alls who discourse learnedly in the bathroom about the technical name for the yellow film on their teeth and use appalling grammar like 'Bags *I* Telly Tots!' Mr Bloggs is so sick of the whole boiling of them that he's usually to be found at the Local, chatting up that gorgeous barmaid who doesn't like the beer she sells but likes the men who drink it.

By now the man from Mars will have seen enough to send him screaming back into space, chewing, no doubt, a chocolate bar thoughtfully named after him.

Well, that's one image of Earthman – beer-swilling husband, self-indulgent wife, chocolate-stuffing children and a dog which consumes more calories per day than two-thirds of the world's human population. Not a very flattering image. I'd hate to think it's the only one on the market. There is another but it's a hard sell, because it's concerned with those who are not hale, hearty nor healthy enough to make good advertising models. It's an image of Man concerned not to offer his neighbour a pint of the best but to secure justice for him – to fight for a system in which none will be excluded from the Feast of Life, even if we affluent have to make do with the odd candy bar less. It's about Man seeking to root out greed and cruelty and to exalt mercy and love.

In fact, it's an image of Man set out in the life and teaching of Sh . . . You Know Who!

Think about it. You *know* it makes sense.

God's Will and Natural Disasters

IT'S A TALL order to attempt to explain natural calamities such as the East Pakistan cyclone in four and a half minutes; not that I think I could do much better if I had four and a half years. The wise keep decent silence and only the foolhardy try to explain the inexplicable.

There are one or two obvious points worth making. Our inability to stave off such disasters in spite of our technological efficiency strikes at our human arrogance and gives us a sharp reminder that we have a long way to go before we can claim to be Lords of the Earth. And I suppose that one could point up the truth that it is at such times that the essential unity of mankind is demonstrated. Without doubt the people of Britain will respond with the utmost generosity to any appeal for aid; just as it is equally beyond doubt that it often takes a tragedy of this magnitude to draw our attention to the plight of the little people of the earth who live on the wrong side of a rich world and who, in terms of our concern, seem to be worth much more dead than alive.

God always gets dragged into discussions about natural calamities. People ask: why does God allow them to happen? It's a curious question because it is so one-sided. If things were going well for us and God intervened to limit our freedom in some way, we would scream outrage and demand the right to go on in our own sweet way free from divine interference. But if things go badly adrift, it's God who gets the blame for not stepping in to stave off whatever might hurt us.

The point is that we are not puppets on a string: we are free agents. The world isn't a clockwork orange in which cause and effect are precisely related. It is a wild thing of beauty and terror, horror and pity, poetry and fire. It doesn't operate according to the laws of exact moral transactions so that good is rewarded by happiness and evil by disaster. As a result, we get benefits we haven't earned and suffering we haven't deserved. These are the rules of the game – no divine interference where either the kicks or the ha'pennies of life are concerned.

So the only explanation of a natural calamity likely to make any sense to us is to be found not in the realms of theology but in the fields of oceanography or meterology or whichever science explains why cyclones and gigantic tides behave the way they do. There's little point in thrashing around beyond our depth trying to read the mind of the God who operates in the ultimate *Why* of things. He's also at work in the immediate *How* of them, and that's much closer to our understanding.

When a tragedy of this order strikes anywhere we may be powerless to prevent human suffering, but we can at least see to it that such suffering is

41

not wasted; that people have not died in vain. And this does not mean more superheated piety to placate some God of vengeance but better civil engineering or weather-prediction. How many victims does it take to jolt us into reassessing our priorities so that we spend less on the rusting ironmongery of war and more on research into the causes of these great scourges of mankind? Who knows: for the cost of a single moon rocket we might beat cancer.

It is not enough to be appalled by the enormity of human suffering in East Pakistan or elsewhere. It's no use looking around for a Divine scapegoat; it's no use wringing our hands and wailing. This world belongs to God but it will be what we make of it. It hasn't slipped out of God's hands; he's freely placed it in ours. That may be a compliment we don't deserve. But one thing is sure. What we do not do through the dedicated and united talents of mankind to stave off natural calamities or ameliorate their worst consequences – what *we* don't do – isn't going to get done.

The Image Makers

I SEE from the press this weekend that a well-known pop group is engaged in what is called changing its image. And last week, Television critics were discoursing solemnly about the effect a documentary might have had upon the public image of a prominent personality.

I must confess to being a little weary of hearing about the so-called public image of personalities and institutions of our society. One of the things most obviously wrong with the modern world is the gap between appearances and reality; between what people seem to be and what they really are. A whole new industry has grown up dedicated to providing a good image for those who can afford to pay for the service. And so skilled are these practitioners that they could dress up some of the Dick Turpins of modern life to look like the Good Samaritan. One is reminded of the story of the African chief who called together his tribe and announced that he had both good and bad news to tell them, 'First, the bad news. The crops have failed and we shall have to live for five years on goat manure. Now, the good news. We have plenty of goat manure.'

Is it really a worthwhile expenditure of time and

skill to give your life to dressing up goat manure so that it smells of *eau de cologne* and tastes of caviare? It is one of our burdens that we have to spend so much time choosing between competing varieties of trash with only glossy images to distinguish them.

It would be a sign of hope for the future of democracy, for example, if a political image and the reality behind it coincided more often. How refreshing it would be if some politicians were to get up and instead of beating us over the head with statistics to prove it was the other lot who wrecked the economy, were to say: 'We've made a hash of things and got right off track. At this moment we haven't the foggiest idea how to get us back but we're going to try.' But, alas, an essential part of the *persona* of the modern politician is that image of imperturbability reminiscent of that parody of Kipling which runs: 'If you can keep your head when all around you are losing theirs, you just don't understand the problem!'

Our society is adept at self-delusion. It will insist on clothing unpleasant realities in fancy wrappings and giving pretty names to ugly realities. There are people who talk of aid when they mean fraud; development when they mean exploitation; inflation when they mean profiteering. And so we can live with a lie provided a wholesome image shields us from a sordid reality.

Our direst need at the moment is not for universal geniuses – they are always in short supply. It is for three dimensional men; men whose image and the reality behind it still coincide when the cameras are switched on and the reporters put away their notebooks and the programme has gone off the air – men who appear what they are and are what they appear and the blazes with their image!

Whenever people say one thing and mean another; whenever they are apt to delude themselves or others, there is urgent need of those who will, as the Americans say, tell it the way it is; who will penetrate the verbiage and rationalisation and uncover the truth. This is a central Christian vocation – to tell it the way it is, pleasant or sordid, nice or nasty – in the belief that every testimony to the truth is a testimony to the one who is the truth. For only the truth can both judge and heal. It is both creative and redemptive. Only from a firm grasp of reality can we move on towards the society of our dreams; only men who see themselves as they truly are can both see the need for and grasp at the possibility of redemption.

There may be more to being a Christian than a steadfast determination to tell it the way it is – there certainly cannot be less.

A Lonely Old Lady and a Half-Starved Dog

HERE ARE two items which did not make the national press this morning – two incidents which occurred not a hundred miles from where I now sit.

An old lady who hadn't been seen for some time was found dead in her bed-sitting-room. Nothing, alas, unusual about that, except that she had been dead for a week and two other families live in that same house and apparently no one had missed her.

And someone drowned an unwanted dog in the local canal. Again, nothing, alas, unusual about this either, except that this worthy citizen, by the exercise of a certain amount of perverted ingenuity had tied to the dog's collar a number of empty, sealed cans by lengths of string so that the animal was neither quite submerged nor yet quite floating; just the tip of his nose broke surface. This ensured that the dog died very, very slowly.

These two stories are important. They announce the fact that we have a long way to go before we can claim the right to call ourselves a civilised nation. In spite of Concorde, the hovercraft, Jodrell Bank and the laser beam, we have still not quite emerged from the Dark Ages.

I don't know by what standards you decide

whether any nation is truly civilised. My yardstick is very simple. How does that society treat those of its members who are not strictly essential to its efficient functioning; who make no economic contribution either by swelling the Gross National Product or helping the export drive? Who just happen to be *there*, and are sometimes an embarrassment or even a nuisance to those responsible for them.

A lonely old lady and a half-starved dog. They are what the industrial economist might call frictional overheads – you get nothing back for any effort you invest in them – except possibly love – a commodity which isn't quoted on the Stock Exchange.

We are told that modern society has outgrown Christianity. To the contrary, incidents like these show that we are in desperate need of the Gospel as a civilising force – not primarily through our great cathedrals or elaborate rituals – but as a message of indiscriminate concern which announces that lonely old ladies and half-starved dogs *matter*.

This is both the power and the difficulty of the way of Jesus – its sheer indiscriminateness. It won't have people pigeon-holed by rank or colour, class or income group. It doesn't set out its stall to attract a special constituency – the floating voter, the average housewife, the higher income bracket. The Gospel states simply that the next person you encounter – across the table, on the street, in the Tube, at the shops – is the inheritor of all the promises of God and so has the right to be cherished. It says that so long as a single old lady can

47

live and die unnoticed there is a fatal flaw at the heart of our economic and social planning, and that weighed in the balance against a single act of neglect all our proud achievements are dust.

Yes, and half-starved dogs too have a place in the economy of God. For those who can look on unmoved as an unwanted animal pathetically struggles for life are the raw material of a society which could countenance the incineration of six million Jews or the obliteration of a quarter of the world's population in a nuclear holocaust.

If it is naïve and sentimental to see the problems of our society in such terms, and if it is bad logic to draw general conclusions from particular cases then I plead guilty on both counts without apology. God preserve us from the so-called sophistication which could take the lonely death of *anybody* or the torture of a dumb animal as a matter of course.

If we can – we are dead, at the level of the soul.

The Greatest Non-Patrial of Them All

TODAY is St David's day. A great man, St David, but I do hope that all Welshmen realize how fortunate he was to have lived before the proposed Immigration Bill becomes law. Some historians say he was born in Cornwall, but there is one tradition which claims that he was born in France. You see the problem. According to the terms of the proposed classification of British residents he would be known as a *non-patrial*, which is someone without a father or grandfather born in Britain. Just think of the poor chap being ferried back and forth across the Channel in a coracle because the King's men would not let him land on British soil.

However, the Welsh are in no worse plight than the rest of us. St George of England probably wasn't a historical figure at all, but if by any chance he was, then he'd give the Immigration people a real headache because he was first heard of in Libya which is where he is supposed to have slain the dragon. This must give rise to the suspicion that he was not only a *non-patrial* but also black. England's patron saint a black *non-patrial*! The mind boggles!

And let no Scotsman adopt a superior attitude. St Andrew was born in Galilee, so he's had it!

This leaves St Patrick of Ireland. By a strange poetic justice, he is the only one of our patron saints whom we can be sure was born in Britain and so qualifies as a *patrial*. Possibly we had all better adopt him quickly.

We may have to take a second look at some of our national heroes in the light of this new legislation. Sir Winston Churchill for example, the greatest Englishman of the Twentieth Century – he was a *patrial*, all right, but his mother was an American – which makes you think. Perhaps we shall need a new companion volume to that admirable reference work *Who's Who*. We could call it *Who's Half-Who*. The England cricket team would have to drop Basil D'Olivera – a fine batsman, but *non-patrial*, alas. And I should think that when some of those excellent West Indian cricketers have been stopped in the street for the tenth time and asked for their passcards they'll be lost to the Lancashire League for ever.

At least this new terminology is going to solve the perpetual problem of the correct name of certain public places – 'Men and Women' is a bit stark; 'Ladies and Gents' is snobbish. We can now label them 'Patrials and Matrials'.

The effect on our tourist industry will have to be considered. Who wants to spend a month roasting on the beach at the Costa Brava and return with a deep, gorgeous tan only to be stopped by a policeman and asked if one has changed one's job and address lately? Still, our culture will be given a new boast. Old rhymes will take on a new significance:

Ten little black boys going down the mine,
One forget his passcard and then there were
nine;
Nine little black boys trying to pull their weight,
One proved to be non-patrial and so there were
eight.

'It's all going to be good clean fun – except for the police of course who will have the unpleasant task of questioning endless processions of perfectly respectable black citizens to catch out the odd dodger. And it isn't going to be much fun either for black residents born here who daren't set foot out of their house without taking their Birth Certificates with them.

For Christians there is the additional problem of having to extend that one-sentence manifesto of Paul's which forms the basis of our judgement of human beings: 'There is neither Jew nor Gentile bond nor free, male nor female, *patrial* or *non-patrial*. All are one in Christ.' That seems to me to be a sounder basis for our national life – the judgement of men by the content of their character rather than their national origins.

I don't subscribe to the view that any Government which proposes legislation with which I cannot agree is composed of fiends incarnate. I'm sure they are honorable and compassionate men, so I hope they'll think again about this Bill – if for no other reason than that it is alien to the spirit of the greatest *non-patrial* of them all – Jesus of Nazareth.

Do It Now!

IF YOU'VE ever lived in the Tropics, you will know that there is a quickening of the pace of life, a growing sense of urgency, when the Rains approach. People say 'We'd better do this, that or the other before the Rains'. Once those torrential storms sweep down, communication becomes difficult, roads and bridges get washed away, valleys and plains are flooded and life is bogged down in the mud until the Rains end.

There's a phrase in Paul's Second Letter to Timothy which breathes this same sense of urgency. Paul, from his Roman jail, asks Timothy, whom he's left in charge of the Church at Ephesus, to visit him, and adds, 'Do your best to come quickly. Come before Winter'. Why 'before Winter'? Presumably because once Winter sets in the Mediterranean becomes unnavigable, and if Timothy delays, it will be Spring before he reaches Rome, and Paul has a feeling in his bones that he may be dead by then.

Before Winter or never. There are some things in this life which will never get done if they are not done before Winter. Certain doors are now open that Winter will close for ever; certain voices to which we can now respond which Winter may silence for ever.

For instance, there is the voice of friendship and affection. If Timothy had delayed, he would have arrived in Rome in the Spring to find his old friend silent in the ground. Some of the saddest words ever put together were inscribed by Thomas Carlyle over the grave of his wife: 'Oh that I had you with me yet for five minutes by my side that I might tell you all.' Whatever Thomas Carlyle had left unsaid, his wife would never hear. Winter had intervened.

It is this certainty that Winter will come which injects urgency into our human relationships. . . . 'What Old Jack gone! I saw him only last week in town.' There was something I intended to say to old Jack when I got round to it; maybe a breach to be healed; words of apology or encouragement to be spoken. But the coming of Winter has mocked my good intentions. Whenever for our peace of mind or our conscience's sake there is something to be said or done for another human being and we decide we will get around to it tomorrow or next week or next month – better think again and do it now, before Winter.

And there is urgency too in the voice of a second chance. Sometimes our personalities are sensitive, malleable, teachable. At other times they are hard, resistant, unresponsive. There are critical times in our lives just as there is a critical temperature at which molten metal can be poured. Let it get too hot or cool down and we can do nothing with it. But strike at the right moment and we can shape as we will. Take the case of a destructive habit or addiction. Before we pass the point of no return, there is always a critical moment when the situation can still be retrieved. An inner voice says 'This is your chance! Master this thing now and you will be free for ever. Delay and you are lost!' Twice in the Garden of Gethsemane Jesus tried to wake his disciples. The third time he said sadly, 'Sleep on' – an irretrievable opportunity had been lost.

So if you are going to make a fresh start, do it now – before Winter.

Supremely, this lesson applies to those times when we are addressed by the voice of God. The uncertainty of human life requires that no opportunity of making our peace with him should be lost. David said to Jonathan, 'There is but a single step between me and death.' There is only one step between *any* of us and death. An old rabbi was asked by his disciples when a man ought to make his peace with God. He thought for a moment and then said, 'A man ought to make his peace with God one minute before he dies.' 'But, Master,' they protested, 'we have no idea when we shall die!' 'Precisely,' said the old man, 'so do it now.'

Do it now. Before Winter.

The Yes Beyond Yes and No

WE ORDINARY citizens are pretty hard on the politicians. We claim that they are purveyors of empty promises; that they always refuse to commit themselves; that they can never be nailed down to an unequivocal answer. We sneer: ask them a simple question and you'll always get the same answer – yes *and* no, with reservations on both sides. But it's just possible that politicians of integrity have learned the hard way that there are few important questions to which a simple answer of yes or no can be returned. Honesty may demand a Yes-But or a No-And-Yet.

Paul seems to understand the politician's dilemma. In one of his letters he describes life as being a blend of Yes and No. Not Yes only. Nor No only. But Yes and No held together in tension. We might not express it so profoundly, but it is an interpretation of life which makes sense.

The search for truth stands under this law of Yes and No. It is a strange fact that in any field if the truth is pursued too rigorously it shades into error. This is the sin of Fascism. It takes a truth about the State and presses it to the point where it becomes a monstrous error.

Man's search for God used to stand under this

55

law of Yes and No. For generations, men have tried to fight their way to God, and many promising paths opened up. A Yes sounded over the human effort to get to heaven by the ways of ritual and renunciation and sacrifice. But at some point along the road, Yes gave way to No. The path was barred. The infinite distance between God and man was protected by a No that could not be got round.

Human achievement stands under this law of Yes and No. Life says Yes to the gifts of a Martin Luther King or a Robert Kennedy, and just when mankind is poised to reap the harvest of their talents this Yes is drowned by a sudden, shocking No, and untimely death steals them from us.

Over the man Jesus, there sounded the clearest Yes history has known. His life was one of ever-broadening horizons in service and healing and teaching. Yet even this sublime Yes was neutralised by the ultimate No of Calvary, and all man's hopes of breaking out of the vicious circle of Yes and No were entombed with him.

Then on the third day, according to the Creed, he rose again from the dead. Another Yes had sounded beyond this historical blend of Yes and No that characterises our natural life. God said Yes to his obedience, goodness and sense of oneness with the source of all life. And this was a Yes that could not be neutralised by the ultimate No of mortality because his death was already behind him. So, as Paul puts it, 'In Christ there is no blend of Yes and No. In him it is always Yes.'

Jesus is God's Yes to a form of truth which is

not balanced out by error. This truth is not speculation or earthly wisdom; it is the saving truth of
the Gospel – truth without error, Yes without No,
because it is truth which can be trusted. You can
stake your life upon it.

Jesus is God's Yes to a discovery of him that is
not barred by any No. A royal road has been
opened to God in which infinite distance has been
annihilated.

And Jesus is God's Yes to a life which is not
cancelled out by mortality's No. Those who live by
the power of his resurrection already have their
death, in any but the biological sense, beyond
them. They live in the realm of a deathless Yes.

But the ultimate dignity of Man and the possible
source of his doom is that the power and potenti-
ality of this great Yes sounded in Jesus can only
be released by our willingness to say our simple
Yes to him. Once that Yes has been uttered, then
any man can stand where Jesus stands – freed from
the crippling law of Yes and No, and in the realm
of a deathless Yes.

Amazing, isn't it, how much can hang, in this
life and beyond it, on that tiny word – Yes?

Decisions! Decisions!

THERE'S a somewhat sick story which runs: two white mice are sitting in the nose-cone of a rocket headed for Mars. 'What a terrible way to die!' sighs one. 'Never mind,' says the other, 'It's better than cancer research.' A somewhat gloomy view of life you might think, in which the only available choice is between the dreadful and the unthinkable. According to the Book of Chronicles, that is the precise choice God once offered David: 'Thus saith the Lord: take what you will; either three years of famine or else three months devastation by your foes; or else three days of the sword of the Lord.'

That cheery word of the Lord to David spotlights one of the key problems of our day – an acute shortage of choices that make much sense. It is the strength of democracy, we are told, that it offers people freedom of choice. That's all very well, but what happens if there aren't different things to choose from?

Certainly, we spend much of our lives making choices, but many of them are false ones ... between Labour's Industrial Relations Bill and that of the Tories; between Mr Callaghan's formula for restricting immigration and that of Mr Maudling.

Indeed, it is one of the mysteries of politics that any measure our side introduces for the good of the country becomes positively harmful if the other side adopts it. Virtually every political policy sonorously uttered seems to contain its own built-in negation. Hence, we have Governments queueing to condemn South Africa at the United Nations and then falling over themselves to trade with her. We found it possible both to sell arms to Nigeria and to send food to Biafra. There are plenty of choices in the political field, but most of them are false ones.

Nor have we in the Churches much cause to look down smugly upon the politicians. Choose between Christ and chaos roars the evangelist to the sob of electronic organ music. Far from being a genuine choice, that is no choice at all. Christ and chaos are not alternatives; they are cause and effect. Take Christ seriously and chaos becomes inevitable, from the undermining of public order to the collapse of the economy. That is why, like the girl who announced that she was slightly pregnant, we prefer to be slightly Christian in the hope that we can *both* follow Jesus *and* keep our two coats. The various Churches seem to offer a bewildering variety of interpretations of Jesus, from the Great Do-Gooder whose only vice is a tendency to steal the humanist's clothes to the Resplendent Warrior in the stained glass armour who broods above the regimental banners in the West Transcept. But do any of them really resemble the Galileean Madman? For make no mistake about it, had Jesus lived in Hogarth's time the gentry would have got

59

up parties to go and laugh at him as they did to
visit the lunatics in Bedlam.

They say life or death is the only absolute
choice. Don't you believe it. Ask any Vietnamese
peasant. He may choose life but along will come
some three-star General to assure him that he is
better off dead than red, or else a Viet Cong com-
missar with a sharp knife to point up the moral
that if he isn't red he *is* dead. On the other hand
choose death if disease turns you into a vegetable
and they'll stick you into a respirator to ensure
you reach your next birthday. As though a vegetable were interested in blowing out candles!

It is said that the choice that really matters will
be made somewhere amidst the computerised efficiency and frightening incompetence of the Pentagon or Kremlin where files get lost, messages go
astray and nuclear alerts sound off by accident.
That, apparently, is the only real decision left; the
one made by the man who presses the red button
which will take the world off its hinges. Even then,
this choice may prove to be a false one. Possibly
the world will end neither with a bang nor a whim-
per but with a muttered exclamation, 'Blast! My
finger slipped!'

And yet . . . the statesman who gives the people
a genuine choice will offer this country a new
lease of life, and the man of God who persuades
men to offer to God the one thing he cannot demand – the human will – must unleash the power
to recreate the world. And, incidentally, they will
also save the truly human person from extinction.

John Wesley and the Belfast Troubles

OVER two hundred years ago, in a time of great religious intolerance, John Wesley wrote this letter to a Roman Catholic. In the light of the present troubles in Northern Ireland, it could hardly be more topical had he penned it yesterday.

'You have heard ten thousand stories of us who are commonly called Protestants, of which, if you believe only one in a thousand, you must think very hardly of us. But this is quite contrary to our Lord's rule, "Judge not, that ye be not judged"; and has many ill consequences, particularly this – it inclines you to think as hardly of us. Hence, brotherly love is destroyed; and each side looking on the other as monsters, gives way to hatred and malice and every unkind affection.

'Now, can nothing be done, even allowing us on both sides to retain our own opinions, for the softening our hearts towards each other, the giving a check to this flood of unkindness, and restoring at least some small degree of love among our neighbours and countrymen? Do you not wish for this? Are you not fully convinced, that malice, hatred, revenge, bitterness, whether in us or in you, in our hearts or yours, are an abomination to the Lord? Be our opinions right or be they wrong, these tempers are undeniably wrong. They are the broad road that leads to destruction, to the nethermost hell.

'I think you deserve the tenderest regard I can show, were it only because the same God hath raised you and me from the dust of the earth, and has made us both capable of loving and enjoying him to eternity; were it only because the Son of God has bought you and me with his own blood.

'In the name then, and in the strength, of God, let us resolve first, not to hurt one another; to do nothing unkind or unfriendly to each other, nothing which we would not have done to ourselves. Rather let us endeavour after every instance of a kind, friendly and Christian behaviour towards each other.

'Let us resolve, secondly, God being our helper, to speak nothing harsh or unkind of each other. The sure way to avoid this is to say all the good we can, both of and to one another: In all our conversation, either with or concerning each other, to use only the language of love; to speak with all softness and tenderness; with the most endearing expression which is consistent with truth and sincerity.

'Let us, thirdly, resolve to harbour no unkind thought, no unfriendly temper, towards each other. Let us lay the axe to the root of the tree; let us examine all that rises in our heart, and suffer no disposition there which is contrary to affection. Then shall we easily refrain from unkind actions and words, when the very root of bitterness is cut up.

'Let us, fourthly, endeavour to help each other on in whatever we are agreed leads to the kingdom. So far as we can, let us always rejoice to strengthen each other's hands in God. Above all, let us take heed to himself (since each must give an account of himself to God) that he fall not short of the religion of love; that he be not condemned in that he himself approveth. Let you and I, whatever others do, press on to the prize of our high calling! that being justified by faith, we may have peace with God through our Lord Jesus Christ; that the love of God may be shed abroad in our hearts by the Holy Spirit which is given unto us. Let us count all things but loss for the excellency of the knowledge of Jesus Christ.'

The present anguish of Northern Ireland may have elements which can be traced to technical matters of politics and economics. And sentiment is no substitute for justice. But one thing is sure. There can be no lasting peace there until all who name the name of Jesus, under whatever label, take to heart the wise words of a man who two hundred years ago, it is claimed, by the power of the Gospel, saved Britain from chaos.

Take Christ Out of Christmas!

CHRISTMAS dyspepsia usually attacks me long before I attack the turkey. I feel the first stab the moment my eye alights on that pathetic slogan 'Put Christ Back into Christmas!' Its weedling tone nauseates me and because it's *wet*, plain *wet*, I know it can have nothing to do with Jesus. It's theological bunkum. As soon plead with the United States Space Administration to put the Sun back in the solar system!

Why on earth ought our society to put Christ back into Christmas? The vast majority of people have rejected his other claims, why should they allow this one? Does the Church think they are masochists or something? They want fun without pain and the modern Christmas gives it to them. The best of luck to one and all! Why sour their festivities by insinuating the 'Helpless Babe' routine into the programme in the hope that what they have flatly rejected in their sober moments they may be prepared to consider in the flush of *bonhommie?*

There is little point in our belly-aching about the commercialisation of Christmas. Maybe we should do the honest thing – take Christ *out* of Christmas. That's the only initiative left to us. We

64

can refuse any longer to garnish a joyous, gorging honest-to-God bout of hedonism with a top-dressing of spiritual justification. Let society find its own justification for living it up.

Let the Church refuse to lend its presence and authority to the mish-mash of heady religiosity which passes for the Christmas spirit. We could refuse the copyright on everything from carols to translations of the Bible, and avoid like the plague baptising with our clerical presence sentimental sing-songs such as Carols by Candlelight. This we should do, not out of spite but to make clear that what we mean by Christmas and what society means can no longer be harmonised.

To make such a suggestion no doubt qualifies me as Wet-Blanket of the Year. So be it. Perverse I may be, but I would claim to be on solid historical ground. For the first four centuries of the Church's life, there *was* no Christmas Day. Throughout the most dynamic and expansionist period of the Christian Mission, no one felt the need to assign a fictious birth-date to Jesus in order to anchor the Incarnation in the calendar. The Early Church celebrated Christmas and Easter every time it assembled.

Why not do the same? Why not make the Christmas celebration part of what Bonhoeffer called 'the secret discipline of the believer'? We spawned this monstrous parody of Incarnation. We owe it to generations yet unborn and some barely alive to try to get rid of it.

Maybe we couldn't take Christ out of Christmas however hard we tried. Possibly there might be a new secular appearance of him because the religious symbols of Christmas, even when cut off from their historical roots, generated a life of their own. Well and good! The other possibility is that the religious dimension of Christmas might contract and disappear, allowing society to revert to the honest celebration of the Winter Solstice. Either possibility is preferable to the present situation.

Certainly, we Christians would suffer most if we adopted such a drastic policy. I shouldn't be surprised if December 25th became the most depressing day of the year. But it would put us on all fours with the majority of mankind who await grimly rather than gladly the arrival of Messiah. It's not that they need redemption any more desperately than the affluent: just that if he should tarry, they won't be around to welcome him.

John Donne once wrote: 'I need thy thunder, O God; thy songs will not suffice me.' That is the sound we might hear in our secret discipline of Christmas which is drowned out by our public celebration of it – the sound of Messiah approaching to establish justice on the earth.

The idea of Messiah as Menace, as a threat to our way of life and possessions is a discordant note to strike in the midst of our Christmas jollification. This is the nub of my objection to *that* slogan. It puts Jesus rather than ourselves on trial.

Maybe Christmas has to be received as Judgement before it can truly be celebrated as Festival.

First Citizen of the Universe

MAN HAS landed on the Moon, and whatever misgivings we may harbour about the cost of the exploit it would be churlish not to salute an incredible feat. This year is unique: quite unlike any in the entire history of the world. Life can never be the same for us again. Now we have to shape up to what it means to be citizens of the universe.

Already, space travel has spawned new arts and sciences. Space biology and medicine, for example, or the codification of laws to govern our journeys to other planets as well as the nature of our claim to extra-terrestial territory. Even our political ideologies are now old-fashioned. Nationalisms are downright parochial and our struggle for true internationalism has become outmoded even before it has found real political expression.

One consequence of becoming citizens of the universe is that besides making new discoveries *out there* we shall find it necessary to reassess many aspects of our life *down here*. Take, for example, that question which has preoccupied visionaries and science-fiction writers for a long time – are we alone in the universe? The implications of the answer to that question – whether Yes or No – are terrifying. And scientists are now facing up to the problems of communicating with any intelligent beings we may discover in outer space. In their search for some non-verbal system of communication, they are turning their attention to that humble and lovable creature of the sea, the dolphin. Dolphins have a more complex brain cortex than that of man and are known to communicate with each other. So marine scientists are observing them with a new respect.

Or take the Bushmen of the Kalahari, amongst the most primitive of men, and almost extinct. Yet they have one faculty which astronauts may find vital – they can live without water for unbelievable periods of time. Then there is the South American lemur which can perform feats of balance which seem to defy the laws of gravity. So astronauts, who have to move around under gravitational conditions quite different from our own, may have much to learn from that tiny jungle creature.

It is truly ironic that our voyage into outer space demands that we look at many aspects of our earthly life through new eyes.

I think the Bible, long discarded as hopelessly unscientific, is about to achieve new significance. For we may find that far from outstripping the reach of its thought we are only now beginning to catch up with it. From its earliest pages, the Bible has described Man as a citizen of the Universe, a veritable Lord of Creation who, in the words of one of the Psalms, has his feet firmly planted in a

68

large room – how large a room it has taken the Apollo Astronauts to demonstrate. And what before might have been written of as a Biblical poetic fancy – ascribing to Man a cosmic dignity – is now a sober fact. So it could be that within the faded covers of that venerable book collecting dust in some forgotten corner of your house there is contained the only adequate philosophy for the Space Age.

Certainly, we would do well to take a much closer look at Jesus. Much that we have found puzzling or inexplicable about his teaching and behaviour may be the result of seeing him against too small a backdrop. The sweep of his vision never seemed confined to this speck of cosmic dust we call the Earth. Suppose what we call his 'miracles' were not spiritual conjuring tricks so much as behaviour normal to Cosmic Man? May it not be that we have our terminology all wrong when we call ourselves human and Jesus super-human? Possibly it is the case that he is truly human and we are still sub-human – not yet fully developed and only using a fraction of the power available within our personalities. Jesus, I believe, was the First Citizen of the Universe – a cosmic trail-blazer, who though he never moved more than a few miles from his birthplace, encompassed the universe in his vision and power.

Sophisticated, scientific Man, trembling on the rim of a much larger world, has everything to learn from this pre-scientific Near Eastern peasant. As Charles Wesley wrote in a great hymn:

> *Soar we now where Christ hath led,*
> *Following our exhalted Head.*

That is now true in more senses than the purely spiritual.

World of Men

I CONFESS to watching no less than three Westerns on Television this week, and I've been trying to analyse their perennial appeal and hypnotic effect as an art form. The soap opera is as stylised as a poem and as polished as one of the parables of Jesus. And it moves to its predictable end with the inevitability of a morality play. Any devotee knows the end from the beginning because he has been weaned on the five variations of the standard plot. He can distinguish the hero from the villain before a word has been spoken, by the cut of his dress, the way he treats his horse or even the style of his saloon-bar leaning. The Western is important because it placards in parody form the dream-life of our society.

The world of the Western is one of bloody innocence in which all men are equal, and the symbol of their equality is the six-gun. The hundred pound weakling if he's quick on the draw is more than a match for the twenty-stone bully. The gun is the basis of civilisation and the guarantor of instant-justice. And the ethic which controls its use couldn't be simpler – you don't draw first and you never ever shoot a woman. Women, of course, occasionally get shot, but that's because of their silly

WHAT THE PAPERS DIDN'T SAY

habit of throwing themselves protectively in front of their lover, when they duly receive the lead aimed at him and expire with a suitably banal cliché on their lips.

All human problems are solved by dispatching them to Boot Hill. No need for psychology, theories of communication, the sheer sweat of human relations. Flying lead resolves all. And in this crazy code of honour, there is only one mortal sin – cowardice, the refusal to draw. It is the willingness to lay your life on the line for a handful of dust which defines true manliness.

There are, of course, type-cast weaklings in the Western; men who will not carry a gun – the preacher, for instance, with beard, Bible and numerous progeny; the doctor who is often a reformed gunman and unreformed drunk and who digs out the bullets to get the show on the road again; and the teacher who fights a losing battle to convince gun-hungry kids that there is another world beyond the foresight of a Winchester.

Things rule supreme in the Western; it is a world where materialism has been carried to its ultimate conclusion. Never an idea, a concept or an abstract value sets the guns thundering. A gold strike, a stage robbery, a battle for land or cattle start the action and pure greed primes the pumps. And because a happy end for our side is mandatory, final resolution is achieved through cataclysm. When things reach the point of maximum complexity then comes the show-down, the gun-fight at the O.K. Corral, and as the smoke finally clears goodness is vindicated and evil vanquished. It is the

72

ethic of the H. Bomb. Little wonder that full-grown Generals stalk the corridors of the Pentagon holstering pearl-handled pistols Western style and growling about using the Big One to bring the North Vietnamese to heel.

Perhaps it's unsporting to take the Western so seriously. But it is the staple diet in celluloid and paper-back of millions so it must prompt for the Christian the serious question: What room would there be in such a world for our hero? When clerks in Battersea bed-sitters dream of reasserting their manhood, eroded by the merciless round of organised boredom, by means of the rope and the rifle; when children learn to draw and fire cap-pistols before they are old enough to be able to read the name on its butt, how can any Gospel which proclaims that it is the meek who inherit the earth take possession of modern man's imagination?

For in the Land of Nod, it is Cain not Jesus who is King.

Eighty Per Cent Water

WELL, the National Census is over, and I wonder whether any of the enumerators had an encounter like that of a counterpart in New York who asked a lady with numerous progeny about her children ... 'Let's see,' she said, 'there's Bill and Fred and Cyril and Mabel and Bessie and Alice and ...' 'Never mind the names,' interrupted the enumerator, 'just give me the numbers.' To which the lady responded with dignity, 'I'll have you know that we haven't got round to giving them numbers yet!' A silly story with a serious point. Has Man a name or is he just a number? Does he count or is he merely counted? That is no rhetorical question in the computer age when the human person is so easily transformed into a hole in a punch card or a series of numbers on a social security file.

It is all too easy to lose Man in the welter of statistics that batter our brains every week – so many thousands killed in war, in road accidents, in natural disasters; so many millions born, most to an anonymous life of hardship and hunger. Historians catalogue Man's national and international acts of savagery and psychologists analyse the dark and sinister drives in his nature. Man badly needs a good word saying for him to help him keep

a good opinion of himself. And the Bible does just
that. It has no doubt about his value or the sacred-
ness of his personality – 'What is Man? Thou hast
made him a little lower than the angels.' That's
the word you need to hear if you are rotting in
some bed-sitting-room, or flowing like one of an
anonymous army of ants out of a factory gate as
the whistle blows or even wasting in luxurious
futility in a Mayfair penthouse. You matter. You
count. You have cosmic dignity.

The blazes with the Naked Ape line! You can
sense something of Man's value in his very con-
struction. Some scientists claim that Man parted
company with the animal world when he first took
hold of a piece of pointed stone and used it as a
tool to extend the range of his hand. Maybe so,
but take a closer look at that hand of yours. It is a
combination of every tool ever invented. It can
perform effortlessly movements that not even the
most complex of machines can match. Or what
about the man who first invented the pump and
was no doubt aghast at his achievement? Yet all
the while inside him was a pump, the human heart,
which circules 280,000 tons of blood a year and
can operate without being serviced for more than
seventy years – *and* it works so silently that it takes
a doctor with a stethoscope to hear it. Or again,
consider that 35-ton computer I saw a while ago
which will multiply 25 figures by 25 figures in five
seconds. Truly amazing, and yet a crude tool in
comparison with the 35-ounce brain which con-
ceived it.

Man may be a speck on a cinder floating in the

immensities of space, but he cannot be lost in those immensities because he alone can measure them. Nor can Man be lost in the animal world. Walt Whitman once wrote a poem about a cow in which he said he would give anything for the contentment of such a creature. Need one comment that although Walt Whitman could write a poem about a cow, no cow could write a poem about Walt Whitman? And it is precisely the dynamic restlessness which Man does not share with the animal world which makes him a poet, a singer and a creator; and also, of course, can drive him to depths of depravity to which no animal could sink.

Nor can you lose Man in materialism. It was H. G. Wells who first pointed out that even the Archbishop of Canterbury is composed of 80 per cent water. So is the Pope, the Prime Minister, the Leader of the Opposition, President Nixon, Mao Tse Tung. So are you. So am I. It's worth remembering that the next time you find yourself afflicted with someone with an over-inflated sense of his own importance. Even He is 80 per cent water, and the other 20 per cent is made up of substances that you could purchase at the chemists for ten bob. 80 per cent water! And yet this being who could apparently have been put together from the ingredients of a child's chemistry set has created civilisations, given to the world great treasures of art and literature and music, and by the use of technology made deserts bloom and released the power locked away in the atom; and most important of all, he can give and receive love.

'A little lower than the angels' – remember that

when the Census takers wave their forms, the computers whirr and attempt to translate your essence into a series of dots on a card. Remember it the next time you get a gas bill that identifies you by a ten figure number and announces that you owe £0000000.00p and had better pay it in seven days or else. Remember it in your moments of loneliness, self-denigration and despair. Whoever you are, and whatever you have done or are unable to do – you do not exist merely to be counted. You count.

What's In a Word?

A FASHION editor wrote the other day that 'Hot pants have become the shibboleth of the swinging set'. I must confess that to my jaundiced middle-aged eye hot pants just look like cold shorts warmed up by super-heated advertising. However, I was intrigued by the use of the word 'shibboleth'. It's not often one finds the Bible quoted on the fashion page of a newspaper. These days the word has come to mean the distinguishing mark of any group of people. But the original story is much more colourful.

According to the Old Testament, there were two warring tribes both descended from Joseph, and each had developed its own particular dialect. The Ephraimites, for example, could not pronounce SH as 'sh ...'. They used the sibilant 'S' One day, a unit of the Ephramites were trapped by their enemy at a ford on the Jordan, and tried to break out by posing as Gileadites. But the wily Jepthath trapped them by choosing as a password 'shibboleth,' which means 'a stream in flood.' The poor Gileadites couldn't pronounce the word properly. They said 'sibboleth' and so speedily got their come-uppance.

It's interesting how much can hang on a single letter of a word. In 1888, Lord Frederick Cavendish, Under-Secretary for Ireland, was murdered in Dublin. And in the House of Commons, a prominent Irish M.P., Charles Stewart Parnell, was accused of being party to the crime, on the basis of a letter approving of the murder and supposedly written by Parnell. This letter had been bought by *The Times* newspaper from a man called Piggot who said he got it in Paris. The drama reached its climax at a judicial hearing when Sir Charles Russell, representing Parnell, questioned Piggot, who was given a piece of paper and asked to spell a number of words. After mentioning several words, Sir Charles Stewart asked Pigott to spell 'hesitancy'. Piggot spelled it with a final 'e' instead of an 'a' – precisely as it had appeared in the letter supposedly written by Parnell. The letter was proved to be a forgery, Parnell was vindicated; Piggot left the witness box and blew out his brains. Just an 'e' and an 'a' saved a distinguished Parliamentary career and prevented a gross injustice being done.

Or take the almost identical terms – *penance* and *penitence*. The Reformation with its tremendous religious and political consequences hung on the difference between those two words. The Church of Luther's day said that 'penance' – the performing of certain prescribed acts was the key to heaven. No, said Martin Luther, not *penance* but *penitence* – an inner disposition of heart, is the thing that really counts. And his insistence upon that extra syllable changed the world.

79

Then there's that vital difference between *reformation* and *regeneration*. Reformation is a sort of ethical change of clothes, whilst regeneration means the remaking of the human personality. And John Wesley unleashed new power and vitality into the life of the world when he stopped preaching the first and rode throughout England proclaiming the second.

There's *might* and *right* – only a single letter to choose between them, but whole civilisations have collapsed in chaos because world leaders have been unable to distinguish between them. So large issues turn upon such tiny hinges.

The ease with which we confuse similar words is more than verbal sloppiness, it exposes our whole philosophy of life. It makes all the difference to our community life, for example, whether we regard the man next door as a *brother* or a *bother*, and the quality of our economic system depends very much upon our willingness to replace *greed* by *need* as top priority.

John Wesley records somewhere in his *Journal* that he once stayed at a country inn and an illiterate serving wench asked him for a simple prayer that she could easily remember. Without hesitation he suggested, 'O Lord, show me myself'. The next time he called there, he found the girl miserable and depressed. And because he was a shrewd old codger, he quickly realized what had happened and made a slight change in the prayer. 'Don't pray, "O Lord, show me *myself*",' he said, 'Pray, "O Lord, show me *thyself*".' Just a tiny alteration, but it released the girl from morbid preoccupation with herself and gave her a new vision and a lively hope.

The change from *myself* to *thyself* is not a mere matter of spelling. It is a decisive shift in the centre of your universe; it is the key to a new life.

Power and Non-Power

POWER – that's the word for our day ... Black Power, Student Power, Nuclear Power, Power-Politics. The title of that television series which starred the late and much lamented Patrick Wymark – The Power Game – is a good short-handed description of life in the modern world. The struggle for power underlies almost every conflict of our day, from the clash of great nations, through industrial disputes to family and marital dust-ups.

A dangerous thing, power, which in our lifetime has devastated the world, torn nations apart and in the process destroyed the personalities of those who have used it wrongly. Yet we can't do without it, for power is the ability to get things done. So we've got to learn to use it.

And it's worth noting that power in essence is ethically neutral. In itself, it's neither good nor bad. It all depends who uses it and how it is used. The cobalt bomb in the hands of a medical specialist can be used to cure cancer; its cousin, the hydrogen bomb, in the hands of a maniac, could destroy the world. Few of us have got *that* degree of power, but all of us have *some* power – in our personal relationships, at work, or in the community. And all of us are on the receiving end of someone else's power. You can make someone else's life miserable by the misuse of power, and you don't have to look far for someone who has the power to turn your life into a fair semblance of hell.

There's one thing we've got to get straight. Power is not an absolute. It is only power*ful* if it is consistent with the declared purpose for which it is intended. The hydrogen bomb is an effective form of power if the purpose is to destroy the world; it is impotent as a means of feeding the hungry. An axe is a power*ful* instrument for chopping down trees but it is slightly less than useful for shaving. Dynamite is a power*ful* device for blasting rocks, but when it comes to lulling a baby to sleep, it is *non*-power. What Paul called 'the power of the Cross' – suffering love – was sheer weakness in the bustling world of Roman power-politics, but it proved immensely power*ful* in changing men's hearts – in melting those who would not break.

In the last resort, there are only two forms of power in this world. Power *over* people (compulsion) and power *with* people (persuasion). And civilisation could be described as man's attempt to replace power *over* people by power *with* people – compulsion by persuasion, regimentation by education.

The classical example of the clash of these two forms of power is seen in the Judgement Hall when Pilate confronts Jesus. Pilate had the power to command men's bodies – the power of death. Jesus symbolised the power to win men's hearts – the power of life. And Pilate was to discover that what he had always believed was the ultimate form of power was really impotence. He could break a thousand men's bodies but could not break one man's spirit.

But as the centuries have rolled on, that poignant lesson has been wasted on us. We still try to use power *over* people to do what can only be achieved by power *with* people. The overbearing parent can use superior force to impose his will on a child, but that power proves impotent to inspire the child to do the right thing willingly. That takes a different form of power, made up of affection, trust and respect – in a word, power *with* the child.

So if power is the ability to accomplish purpose, then we ought to look closely again at the Cross as the ultimate form of power in doing what God intends for the world – winning the loyalty of men without violating their freedom.

And I suspect that when we get down to the thorny question of deciding what our ultimate purposes are – such as creating a just and peaceful society, and of passing on to our children a world in which they can be more fully human and where all men can take their place at the Feast of Life, we shall discover that what we have often regarded as the power to achieve these ends turns out to be *non*-power, and what some men sneer at as the ultimate weakness – the way of suffering love, will prove to be the ultimate power.

Certainly, in a mad, mixed-up world, suffering love is the only form of power which can do men good without an inevitable backlash of harm.

That Bald Cliché

WE ARE in the throes of yet another national strike; inflation is increasing by leaps and bounds, and the morale of our people is at a pretty low ebb. I note that one public personality, writing to a national newspaper, has somewhat sardonically asked what the Church has to say about the present situation beyond 'the bald cliché that God is love'?

I personally would not be quite so swift to dismiss the affirmation that God is love as a 'bald cliché'. Nonetheless his question is a fair one, and we Christians would be the first to admit that a number of aspects of this crisis concern technicalities of economics and politics about which our views are no more weighty than anyone else's. Certainly, any comments we are to make in these fields must be judged on their merits and not ascribed a magical authority as though we had exclusive power to read the mind of God.

But one truth we Christians can state roundly is that the root of our problems is not to be found in questions of political organisation or economic policy. Society is sustained in the last resort by mutual respect and trust amongst its members. It is governed by the operation of laws which are hidden and often unformulated, and society cannot be fundamentally changed for the better by shifts in policy, but only by a transformation of the consciousness of the people. This is another way of saying that salvation does not come by way of analysis, however profound.

No amount of subtle analysis can take account of a factor which is always operative in society and generally passes undetected – a deep corruption of the human will which is the cause of some problems and bedevils many more. So any dangerously divided society, and ours most certainly is, requires a *gospel* of reconciliation, which is always more than a matter of personal spiritual renewal. It also involves the search for institutions which can contain human frailty and even harness our natural weaknesses for benevolent ends.

The Christian Gospel of Reconciliation, which has its origin in that 'bald cliché' – God is Love, has many insights that bear upon our present troubles. One is the power of imagination by means of which we can put ourselves in someone else's shoes and see how our actions and policies look from the wrong side of the Bread Line, or the ghetto quarter of the city. This faculty ought also to enable us to look out through the windows of 10 Downing Street and if the Government is not one which we elected, prevent us from ascribing demonic powers to politicians wrestling with problems calculated to baffle the best brains of the day.

No less important is the Christian compulsion to *hear* and *see* those whose views differ from our own. At present, employers and workers seem to be shouting past each other. They do not *hear* what the opposing group is saying. A willingness to listen, and an openness to the justice in the other man's case may seem a very elementary response to a situation of great complexity, but it is vital to that acknowledgement of our opponent's integrity without which social life is impossible.

By the same token, we are prone to look at other groups within society without *seeing* them. Those on the other side of the cultural, racial or class barrier, cease to be individuals and become stereotypes. In racial terms, for example, a white criminal is just a criminal, but a black criminal becomes one more evidence of the anti-social nature of his whole group. The trade unionist in conflict with his employers is seen as an agent of a conspiracy against society, generally communist inspired, rather than a fellow-citizen concerned about the future of his wife and family.

Or consider the highest exercise of human love – the forgiveness of our enemies. There are politically redemptive possibilities in the exercise of a degree of forebearance which enables us to disagree with our fellowmen without hating them. And forgiveness is not solely a quality which sets us right with God; it also links us to all those with whom we share the solidarity of guilt. For God knows, we've done our bit to increase inflation and intensify social conflict by our regard for our own interests at the expense of those who have not the same power to protect themselves.

What that 'bald cliché' really teaches us is that our nation's main engagement is with God and not

with an economic crisis or a political dilemma.
And the attempt to see things from a God-ward
point of view offers an independent standing
ground from which we can do better than offer
mere justice to our opponents. We can cherish
them. It is this insight alone which can transform
the consciousness of the people and so change
society for the better.

The Loneliness of the
Long-Distance Runner

TODAY is the birthday of probably the most anonymous of the great men of the twentieth century,
Dag Hammarskjold, late Secretary-General of the
United Nations Organisation. All senior civil servants are elusive characters. They must cultivate
unobtrusiveness to avoid up-staging their more
flambuoyant political masters. They exercise
power in private, away from the glare of the television lights and the clamour of the public meeting. The top international civil servant has a
unique problem because his master is not one
Minister or even a single Government. He serves
a whole galaxy of Governments, many of whom
are deeply divided from one another on policy
and ideological grounds. So he must walk the
narrow line which divides discretion from paral-
ysis.

I'm not concerned with the great achievements
of Dag Hammarskjold – his struggle to advance
the frontiers of international cooperation; his
crusade to limit the power of the great nations
and to maximise the power of the U.N.; his determination to give new dignity to weak and small
nations; and his inspired use of the medium powers as peace-keeping forces to avoid a confrontation

between the super-States. I want to concentrate upon one simple but often unnoticed characteristic of those who must move in the areas of great power – their loneliness.

Hammarskjold was a bachelor. In a rare moment of personal confession, he said that he had never married because of the price his mother paid, being married to a Prime Minister who had to sacrifice his family life to constant preoccupation with great affairs of State. There are privileges and burdens in the exercise of great power; we do well to remember that behind most men of power there is a family paying some price in loneliness for his eminence and service.

There was another reason for Hammarskjold's loneliness. He dare not draw his friends from either East or West for fear of compromising his impartiality. Everyone knows where the national statesman stands. His loyalty, first, last and all the time is to his own country, so he can even afford friendships across ideological barriers. But the first citizen of the international community, living in an atmosphere of almost paranoid suspicion, is denied the indiscriminateness of ordinary affection. Hammarskjold only partially solved the problem by seeking his friends amongst the only real international community, the world of the arts.

Even his religion was an intensely private thing. Because many faiths and none are represented in the U.N., Hammarskjold avoided public commitment to the religion of the West. He had to find spiritual power within himself and in the world of action. Three months before he died in a plane crash whilst leading a peace mission in the Congo, he wrote these words:

> *Tired*
> *And lonely*
> *So tired*
> *The heart aches.*
> *Meltwater trickles*
> *Down the rocks,*
> *The fingers are numb,*
> *The knees tremble.*
> *It is now,*
> *Now, that you must not give in.*
>
> *On the path of the others*
> *Are resting places,*
> *Places in the sun*
> *Where they can meet.*
> *But this*
> *Is your path,*
> *And it is now,*
> *Now, that you must not fail.*
>
> *Weep*
> *If you can,*
> *Weep,*
> *But do not complain.*
> *The way chose you –*
> *And you must be thankful.*[1]

As we salute his memory, we remember thankfully all anonymous soldiers of peace who must

[1] Hammarskjold, *Markings*, p.175 [Faber 1964].

endure what might be called (to use the title of a recent best-selling novel) the loneliness of the long-distance runner ... those who forge ahead of mankind, charting its path; their loyalty to an abstraction which they seek to bring to birth – truly international community.